PenHero Quarterly

Q2 2017

by Jim Mamoulides

PenHero.com LLC
2017

PenHero Quarterly

Copyright © 2017 by Jim Mamoulides / PenHero.com LLC

All rights reserved. This book or any portion thereof may not be reproduced or used in any manner whatsoever without the express written permission of the publisher except for the use of brief quotations in a book review or scholarly journal.

All photographs in this book are copyright © 2017 by Jim Mamoulides / PenHero.com LLC

Volume 1, Issue 2
First Printing: 2017
ISBN 978-0-9990510-1-6

PenHero.com LLC
Post Office Box 99626
Raleigh, NC 27624-9626
www.PenHero.com

Acknowledgements

Special thanks to my amazing wife Barb, who read every word of this book, patiently making it a better read and for her invaluable help with photo composition

Thanks to Stan Klemanowicz for his invaluable expertise and insights on the Japanese pens presented in this book

Thanks to the Chikazawa Collection of Kochi, Japan for loaning the pens featured on pages 27, 35-38, 49-52, 58-59, 78-79, and 96

Thanks to Andy Lambrou for providing Classic Pens and Lambrou Pens examples, especially prototype pens, for photographs

Contents

- Acknowledgements ... 3
- Forward ... 5
- Aikin Lambert, USA ... 6
- Aurora, Italy ... 7
- Classic Pens, USA and United Kingdom ... 8
- Cleo Skribent, Germany ... 17
- Conklin, USA ... 18
- Crocker, USA ... 25
- Giuliano Mazzuoli, Italy ... 26
- Ikoma, Japan ... 27
- Jumbo Pen, Japan ... 28
- Mabie Todd, USA and United Kingdom ... 29
- Marukin, Japan ... 35
- Morgan nib pen, Japan ... 37
- Morison nib pen, Japan ... 38
- Parker, USA and United Kingdom ... 39
- Platinum silver leaf pattern pen with contemporary copies, Japan ... 49
- Popura, Japan ... 52
- Porsche Design, Germany ... 53
- Postal, USA ... 55
- Recife, France ... 56
- Sager, USA ... 57
- Sailor, Japan ... 58
- Seishi Bosatsu kamakura-bori Japanese art pen ... 59
- Sheaffer, USA ... 60
- Swan, Japan ... 78
- Steady nib pen, Japan ... 79
- Tuckersharpe, USA ... 80
- Uetosi, Japan ... 81
- Wahl Eversharp ... 82
- Waterford, USA ... 87
- Waterman, USA and France ... 88
- Wearever, USA ... 90
- Well, Japan ... 95
- Yotsubishi, Japan ... 96
- Manufacturers ... 97
- Glossary ... 99
- References ... 100
- About the Author ... 100

Forward

This second issue profiles ninety-one pens from thirty-four different pen makers, one for each day of the month from April through June.

A special focus of this book is on the continuous improvement of the portable fountain pen from its beginnings as a nib attached to a barrel full of ink. As you read, you will discover threads of the story of design changes and engineering that began with dip pens and eventually developed to the modern cartridge pen. Fourteen different ways to fill a pen are represented, and though it sounds like a lot, many other methods are not covered in this book. Consider this a sampler. There is a section in the Glossary to explain all of the ones included.

This book also provides a sampler of the many different sizes, shapes and materials used over a period of 135 or more years. The early cylindrical hollow rubber ink stick with a nib became streamlined, faceted, and overlaid. Exciting ebonites, plastics and metals, plain or decorated with carvings, guilloche engraving, urushi lacquer, show the creativity applied to artistic and commercially made pens. There is a pen for every taste.

Note the variety of nibs represented. Most are familiar with the classic "open" nib, a fingernail that conveys ink to the page. Sheaffer in particular innovated in this area, designing the conical Triumph nib in the 1940s and the Inlaid nib in the late 1950s.

This book is intended to give you one pen and its story each day. Each was selected so there would be something new to see, even for seasoned collectors. I hope you enjoy it!

Jim Mamoulides
August 15, 2017

Aikin Lambert retracting dip pen and magic pencil combination c1880s

Aikin Lambert was founded in New York City to make gold pen nibs sometime after the Civil War. The company began to make fountain pens in the 1880s. This Aikin Lambert gold filled retracting dip pen and magic pencil combination was made most likely in the 1880s and is complete with the original box. Fully open, as shown, the small writing instrument is only 4 7/8 inches long. Closed, it's a tiny 2 11/16 inches.

It's used like a quill pen, dipping the nib in ink and writing until the nib dries out. The nib extends by pushing the slider, the raised band with the flat knurled design. A slot runs the length of the opposite side of the barrel where a tab attached to the slider connects to the nib holder. Moving the slider brings the nib into and out of the barrel. The barrel engraving is a checkerboard design. The flexible gold nib is not hallmarked, so the gold content is not known. It's stamped indicating an Aiken Lambert Number 4 medium nib. Many different nibs would have been available. The magic pencil extends and retracts by twisting the knob on the opposite end from the nib.

Aurora Firenze Special Edition sterling silver c2007

The Firenze is a tribute to Aurora's home town of Florence, Italy, the "Cradle of the Italian Renaissance." The high relief .925 sterling silver cap overlay depicts the Ponte Vecchio, Michelangelo's David, the Cathedral, and the Palazzo della Signoria, with a cap band adorned with the Florentine fleur de lis, the symbol of the city of Florence. The Terra di Toscana resin barrel has a repeating pattern of imprinted Florentine fleur-de-lis, which is red with the stamens showing between the petals, thus the red color of the barrel and also appeared on the fiorino, the currency of Florence. The piston filling fountain pen is about 5 ¼ inches long with the cap on, featuring an 18 karat gold rhodium plated nib in multiple grades, and retailed for $1,650.00. Matching rollerball and ballpoint pens were made. Aurora also made the Firenze in vermeil (gold plate over sterling silver) and 99 in solid gold.

Classic Pens CP1 Targa by Sheaffer 1990

The first series in the Classic Pens CP Collection, the CP1, was launched in 1990. Developing the CP1 brought together Classic Pens, Sheaffer and the Murelli R S.A.R.L. engraving company of France to create an exclusive Vannerie (basketweave) pattern on the sterling silver Sheaffer Targa cartridge / converter fountain pen with gold plated trim. The popular Targa by Sheaffer was launched in 1976 and is regarded as a modern classic. It is 5 ¼ inches long with the cap on.

The CP1 Targa was offered in an edition of 250 pens, each laser engraved on the cap ornament with the CP1 logo and the individual limited edition number. The cap band is engraved with the Sheaffer name and the pens carry the London Assay Office sterling silver mark. The standard nib offered was a medium 14 karat gold nib, but any Targa nib could be exchanged onto this pen. Originally sold in Sheaffer gift boxes, when new burgundy handmade boxes were created for the CP2 in 1993, handmade red boxes were created for the last 100 CP1s available for sale. These new boxes won first prize at the London Olympic Exhibition. The CP1 has increased significantly in value over time.

Classic Pens LR1 Eagle Chief by Paul Rossi on the Parker Duofold 2001

Classic Pens LR series is a set of five museum quality art pens created by Paul Rossi in 2001. The first pen in the series, the Eagle Chief, Paul Rossi created .925 sterling silver overlays on the cap and barrel of a black Parker Duofold Centennial fountain pen. The high relief, detailed engravings on the overlay artwork showcase the head of a Native American Chief in full feather head dress on the barrel, framed Native American symbols. The eagle was a favorite theme, and is depicted on the cap overlay in flight with the full sun in the background, hence the title Eagle-Chief.

Paul Rossi and Andy Lambrou met for the first time during the Los Angeles Pen Show in 1991. Later, Paul Rossi put together some of his silver filigree work, including a Native American warrior with one feather, to demonstrate what type of work he could do for Classic Pens. Andy Lambrou showed the Paul's work to the Parker Pen Company in England and they authorized the Duofold Centennial for the LR Collection. This pen marked the beginning of a long term working relationship between them and the two continue to create exclusive art pens.

Classic Pens LR2 Harvest by Paul Rossi on the Parker Duofold 2001

The second in the series, Paul Rossi created the Classic Pens LR2 Harvest fountain pen on the Red Jasper Parker Duofold Centennial fountain pen. The sterling silver overlay on the cap and barrel is based on an original watercolor of wheat, grapevines, and morning glory flowers, reminiscent of harvest time on Cyprus.

The 5 silver filigree designs LR1-LR5 were launched at the Los Angeles Pen Show February 2001. All six LR pens are shown at the right.

Classic Pens LR3 Woodland Oak by Paul Rossi on the Parker Duofold 2001

The third in the series, Paul Rossi created the Classic Pens LR3 Woodland Oak fountain pen on the Green Jade Parker Duofold Centennial. The .925 sterling silver overlay artwork evokes American Oak, with a high relief and detailed design of oak leaves and acorns.

Paul Rossi's hallmark can be seen at the top of the barrel overlay. The 925 hallmark can be seen in an oval on both overlays.

Development work on the Classic Pens LR sterling silver overlays by Paul Rossi started early in 2000. By the end of that year, 5 designs were created, ten pens in each design: the Eagle Chief, Harvest, Woodland Oak, Muse, and Alaska. All were released in 2001.

PenHero Quarterly
Classic Pens LR4 Muse, by Paul Rossi on the Parker Duofold 2001

For the fourth in the series, Paul Rossi created the Classic Pens LR4 Muse fountain pen on the Jasper Red Parker Duofold Centennial. The .925 sterling silver overlay artwork on the barrel is the Muse of Sculpture.

This one showcases the tremendous detail Paul Rossi puts into his sterling silver work. The high relief engraving depicts the Muse's head and her long flowing hair, with flowers in it. The cap overlay is an intricate web of flowers on their stems, woven together.

Classic Pens LR5 Alaska by Paul Rossi on the Parker Duofold 2001

The Classic Pens LR5 Alaska, completing the series, was made by Paul Rossi on the Lapis Blue Parker Duofold Centennial fountain pen. The sterling silver overlay work depicts a lake and forest scene with mountains in the background.

The .925 sterling silver overlay artwork on the barrel depicts an American Bald Eagle at its nest with two eaglets. It's a family of eagles, with the male in flight with the sun. The cap overlay is a highly detailed mountain scene with a lake at the front, pine trees along its edge and the mountains in the background. The image is framed by a foreground pine tree whose branches are covered in fans of needles.

The first five pens in the LR series were featured in the May/June 2001 issue of PenWorld. The Parker Duofold Centennial used as the basis for these pens is 5 3/8 inches long and is a cartridge / converter pen.

Classic Pens LR Lighthouse by Paul Rossi on the Parker Duofold 2001

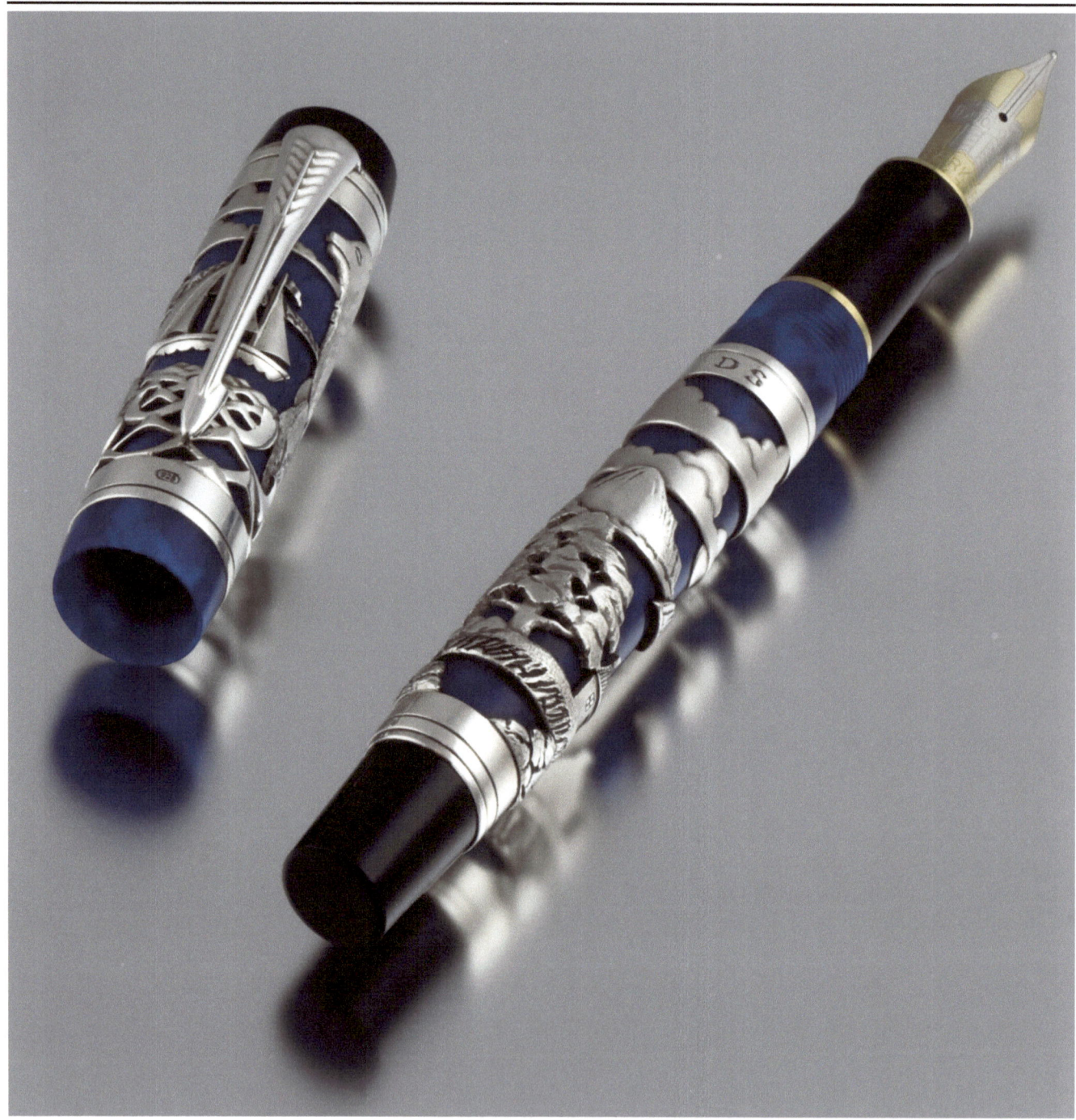

The Classic Pens LR Lighthouse is a one of a kind art pen, created as a gift, based on a stained glass artwork design of a lighthouse and sailing ship. Paul Rossi crafted the .925 sterling silver overlays on a Lapis Blue Parker Duofold Centennial fountain pen. The artwork depicts a coastal scene with a lighthouse on the barrel overlay and a sailboat on the cap overlay. Paul Rossi added a seal on the barrel artwork to complete the design.

The Parker Duofold Centennial was the top of the line Parker pen in 2001, a suitable canvas for the LR art pens. The modern Duofold was introduced in 1987 to celebrate the Parker's 1988 Centennial year and to celebrate the original Duofold pen, introduced in 1921. The Duofold is quite large at 5 1/4 inches long with the cap on and 6 ½ inches long with the cap posted on the end of the barrel. Parker handcrafted each finely engraved platinum plated two tone 18 karat gold nib for the pen in a large selection of nib grades. Parker Duofold fountain pens are noted as excellent writers, making these art pens suitable for everyday use.

Classic Pens LS 11 Nihonrisu (Squirrels) maki-e on the Parker Duofold 2004

The Classic Pens LS 11 Nihonrisu (Squirrels) is a high relief maki-e design on the Parker Duofold Centennial released in 2004.

Squirrels symbolize trust. They may be friendly, playful, and energetic, but they also store up for the future. The togidashi (burnished) and taka (raised) maki-e artwork shows a pair of playing squirrels on a tree surrounded by leaves. The artist, Shogetsu Mitani, created a textured finish on the pen body making it resemble tree bark, as if the pen was the trunk of a tree.

Togidashi maki-e is a maki-e technique where an urushi lacquer painting is sprinkled with gold or silver powder and then painted to fix the powder. Taka maki-e is a maki-e technique where the design is built up from the surface or literally "raised."

The Nihonrisu (Squirrels) maki-e design was offered as 15 pieces on the Parker Duofold Centennial as a 2004 Limited Edition.

Classic Pens LS 12 Shimarisu (Chipmunks) maki-e on the Parker Duofold 2004

The Classic Pens LS 12 Shimarisu (Chipmunks) is a high relief maki-e design highly complementary to the LS 11 Nihonrisu, where the squirrels are replaced by chipmunks. It is shown here on the Parker Duofold Centennial and was released in 2004. The LS 11 Nihonrisu (Squirrels), LS 12 Shimarisu (Chipmunks) and the LS10 Inochi (Life) designs work together as a three pen set.

Chipmunks also symbolize trust. They are curious and playful, and they represent a balance between trust and caution as well as flexibility in one's opinion. Chipmunks, if they trust you, will climb into your hand to eat seeds. The togidashi (burnished) and taka (raised) maki-e artwork shows a pair of playing chipmunks on a tree surrounded by leaves. The artist, Shogetsu Mitani, created the textured tree bark finish on the pen body.

The Classic Pens LS 12 Shimarisu (Chipmunks) maki-e design was offered as 15 pieces on the Parker Duofold Centennial as a 2004 Limited Edition.

Cleo Skribent Linea. Arte c2005

The Cleo Skribent Linea. Arte series is an homage to the 1930s Art Deco metalwork designs by the Fend Company, founded in Pforzheim, Germany. Pforzheim is known for its high quality jewelry and watch-making industry, earning the nickname "Goldstadt" or Gold City. Fend, well known for making jewelry quality metal mechanical pencils. made the likely inspiration for this design, the 1930s faceted Fendograph fountain pen. Art Deco started in France just before World War I and became popular in the 1920s and 1930s, impacting the visual arts, architecture and design.

The Linea. Arte pen line consisted of a fountain pen, ballpoint pen and pencil, made of solid .925 sterling silver. The clip is silver-plated. The nib is rhodium plated 18 karat gold and was available in fine, medium and broad. The pen is 5 ¾ inches long with the cap on. The price of the fountain pen in 2005 was 154 €, the most expensive pen Cleo Skribent offered at the time. The matching ballpoint pen and 0.7 mm mechanical pencil were 77 € each.

PenHero Quarterly
Conklin Symetrik Endura Leaf Green c1930-1931

Conklin added the Symetrik name to its streamlined Endura pens in the 1930-1931 catalog. Clearly a response to the 1929 Sheaffer Balance, the Symetrik Endura echoed several design elements of the Balance in a rather Conklin way. The cap and barrel shape is more blunted than the Balance. Where Sheaffer's top pens had the White Dot, Conklin gave the Symetrik Endura a gold Conklin Crescent inlaid above the clip on the cap. The Conklin had two cap bands instead of Sheaffer's single wide band. The 1930-1931 Symetrik Endura pens were offered in two finishes, "Black and Gold" and "Leaf Green," and in three sizes, long, medium, and a short ringtop pen. This one, the long version, 5 3/16 inches with the cap on, sold for $8.00, while the smaller sizes sold for $6.00. Each size had a matching pencil for $4.00 and $3.50.

Although this Conklin is rather discolored and suffers plating loss, it has the correct nib and the barrel imprint is strong. A great example of a quality worry-free daily user pen, free from concerns about further degrading the appearance.

Conklin Nozac Word Gauge Black c1934-1935

Conklin Nozac pens have become collector items, very likely due to the appealing combination of the piston filling unit and the fact Conklin used very eye-catching celluloids. Conklin was one of the first companies to bring a piston filler to market in 1931 and advertised that it filled like "winding a watch." It works by twisting the knob on the end of the barrel, activating a mechanical piston inside that draws in ink through the nib similarly to a syringe.

Word Gauge Nozacs have a completely clear upper barrel marked in a scale to 5,000 (5M) or 7,000 (7M) words (each thousand marked with an 'M') indicating the number of words that the remaining ink could write. The 7M pen is the "oversize" Nozac, and the 5M is the "standard" size, both the same length. Caps have two or three narrow cap bands, and early pens have a gold crescent inlay above the clip and on later pens it's below the clip, as shown in a 1935 catalog. Eleven nib grades were offered. They were about 5 3/8 inches long and 7000 word fountain pens sold for $7.50, 5000 word models sold for $5.00, and matching twist action pencils were $3.50.

Conklin Endura Reptilian Pearl Gray c1934

Conklin used this snakeskin celluloid called Reptilian Pearl from 1934 to 1938. It was used on their All American pen line in 1937. Conklin appears to have dropped the Endura name from use by 1935, calling their lever fill pens simply "sac pens" and emphasizing the Nozac piston filler as the top product. By 1935, Conklin was putting the gold Crescent inlay below the clip only on the Nozac. Given those clues, and that this one has the Endura barrel imprint, a Conklin Crescent lever, and a gold inlaid Conklin Crescent below the clip, it dates to c1934. The pen is 5 1/8 inches long with the cap on.

The snakeskin celluloid came in three colors, Reptilian Pearl-Gray, Reptilian Gold-Green Vein, and Reptilian Foliage-Red Vein. Conklin offered their top line with a wide choice of 14 karat gold nib grades: extra fine, fine, medium, coarse (broad), and stub medium, stub broad, left oblique, two way, and Recorder in extra fine, fine and medium. Endura pens retailed for $7.00 and $5.00 in 1934.

Conklin Chicago pen c1938-1943

The Conklin Fountain Pen Company was sold in 1938 and production moved to Chicago. The new Chicago based company focused on less expensive pens and the high quality of the Conklin brand declined over time. Some earlier Conklin Chicago lever fillers appear to be made from parts brought from the Toledo, Ohio factory with a Chicago barrel imprint. Other, later pens, such as this 5 3/8 inches long one, show new materials and design and that they were capable of high quality.

This one looks similar to the later Conklin Glider, including the striped celluloid cap and barrel, the Cushon Point nib and the visulated section. The barrel has the Conklin Chicago imprint and it's a much higher quality build than the Glider. The gold plating is on par with earlier Toledo, Ohio made pens. The cap, barrel and section materials are higher quality and better finished than the Glider. The sharper taper to the cap and barrel, the 3/8 inch wide ribbed cap band and the narrow spring loaded clip are quality touches and indicate possibly that the company was aiming at the market leading Sheaffer Balance. Given the design and quality, it pre-dates the Glider, probably c1938-1943.

Conklin Glider c1944-1946

The Conklin Glider was the last quality product by the once market leading company, but a definite step down from the Toledo, Ohio and early Chicago made pens. Gliders have the attributes of second tier pens like Weavers, including lightly gold plated trim that easily wears off, loose fitting cap bands, and twisted or distorted cap and barrel celluloids.

Two things make Gliders of interest to collectors. First, Gliders came with the excellent Conklin Cushon Point 14 karat gold nib. Many Gliders are found with replacement stainless steel nibs, with the original nib probably taken and used as a replacement on more expensive older Conklins. Second, Conklin still had access to and used interesting celluloids for the cap and barrel. Conklin called the striped celluloid on the Glider "dichro-plastic" striped inlay patterns. At least four colors were offered, including green, red, blue and gold stripe. Glider fountain pens are 5 inches long and sold for $2.75, with the matching pencil for $1.20.

Conklin Glider c1944-1946

The Conklin Glider was made in three versions, though only one version was shown in Conklin advertising. This is the largest pen, which also has a wide cap band. All three Glider versions are the same length. The difference is in barrel and cap width, with only the largest model having a wide cap band. The two narrower versions are visually identical, but can be identified easily as the caps will not swap. It's unknown if there was any premium for the larger pen with the wide cap band. The section on this pen may be a replacement, as it does not have the clear ink view feature.

A Conklin advertisement from 1944 describes the Glider as a new fountain pen featuring the 14 karat gold Cushon Point nib and selling for $2.75 and $3.95 in a set with the matching pencil. The new Glider features a clear Visink section and was available in "dichro-plastic" striped inlay patterns. Other advertisements from 1944 to 1946 show it offered in four striped colors.

Conklin Glider c1944-1946

This Conklin Chicago made pen has the hardware and design of the standard size Glider, but there are no advertisements or catalog information showing the Glider was made in this material. Underneath where the gold plate is wearing off, the metal appears to be silver, indicating production during World War II when brass was limited to the war effort.

The cap and barrel material is alternating strips of black and cream lizard skin similar to the Reptilian Pearl used on Conklin Toledo pens from 1934-1938 and a mint green pearlized material divided by black stripes. This same material was used by Eagle on their top of the line c1939 Prestige. Conklin's 1944 advertisement introducing the Glider gives a hint that they may have used more than striped celluloids on the Glider, saying the pens were available in "many smart color combinations." The nib is probably a replacement as a Conklin Cushon point nib would be expected.

Two Crocker Ink-Tite pens c1910s

The Crocker Pen Company was founded in 1902 in Boston, Massachusetts, by Seth Sears Crocker, and later moved to New York City. Crocker is noted for interesting designs, particularly for its Ink-Tite blow filler pens, patented in 1901 and 1904. They fill by dunking the nib section into an inkwell and either blowing into or attaching and compressing a bulb at the hole at the base of the barrel. This squeezes the ink sac, which fills as it decompresses. There is a concave depression in the top of the cap and in the bottom of the barrel and each has a hole drilled at the center. The cap can be used to lengthen the pen for this purpose. One would need to be careful filling the pen so as not to blow ink out of the bottle and wind up with an inky mess.

These two Croker's are exceptional examples, about 5 ¼ inches long and both have friction fit slip on caps. The mother of pearl shell overlay pen has one slightly open joint between two of the panels. The mottled red hard rubber is an exceptional vibrant color. Unfortunately, one is missing the original nib and the other one's 14 karat gold nib is a damaged. Prices in 1915 started at $2.50 for a black hard rubber model.

Giuliano Mazzuoli Moka 3 in 1 fountain, rollerball and ballpoint pen c2008

Italian designer Giuliano Mazzuoli got the inspiration for the Moka pen from his memories of his grandmother's kitchen in the 1950s. She kept four or five different size Moka espresso-makers hanging on the wall. The Moka stove top espresso maker, designed and produced by Alfonso Bialetti in 1930 is still made today. Like the Moka pot, the Moka pen is made of two faceted pieces that screw together creating a narrow waist at the joint.

This black Giuliano Mazzuoli Moka 3 in 1 fountain, rollerball and ballpoint was available in 2008. The pen converts by unscrewing and replacing the nib unit with a rollerball section cap that can take specially modified rollerball and ballpoint refills. All necessary conversion parts are included in the box. The Moka is a large, slender international type cartridge / converter pen 5 5/8 inches long with the cap on. The medium nib is two-tone 18 karat gold. In 2008, there were five versions of the Moka, in black resin, red resin, petrol blue anodized metal, brushed chrome plated aluminum, and polished chrome plated aluminum, all retailing for $375. The Limited Edition Senza Titolo version retailed for $1,000.

Ikoma eight-sided silver pen c1939

Ikoma was a famous jewelry shop in Osaka. Founded in 1870 by Gonkichi Ikoma as a jewelry and watch workshop, G. Ikoma Ltd. was established in 1923 and moved into the landmark Ikoma Building in 1930. The Ikoma building, designed by Heizo So, still stands today as an Osaka historical building.

This 5 inch long eight-sided silver Japanese pen was made by Ikoma, probably c1939 and is a similar faceted design as the Fendograph fountain pen made by Fend in the 1930s. The clip is stamped Ikoma-sei, "Made By Ikoma."

It has a flexible steel Falcon type nib that dates it to the late 1930s because gold nibs were not used in Japan after about 1939. The band at the base of the cap is ebonite.

Cigar shape Jumbo Pen with Perfect gold plated nib c1950s

This is a huge Japanese eyedropper filling pen measuring 6 3/8 inches long with the cap on and just under an inch across at the cap band. The pen can be posted, if you want to write with a pen that's 7 3/4 inches long. Several resources point to two types of these extra-large hachi-bu (24mm diameter) pens. First are high quality, even maki-e decorated pens and the other are no-name inexpensive / export pens. Both were made in flat top and cigar shape designs. A pre-war High Class Nine Fountain Pen catalog that shows two similar jumbo pens with 14 karat gold nibs. The balance shaped pen's name translates as "Cigar Shape Jumbo." Similar ones are shown in post war catalogs, such as the 1957 Yotsubishi, which shows an elaborate maki-e pen. This size was not always a novelty or cheap product.

Similar examples were imported to the US in the 1930s with a selling price of 99 cents. There are no maker's marks, and because the feed is newer and has a gold plated PERFECT stainless steel nib, it could be pre or post World War II. The nib writes surprisingly well, with a wet medium line.

Mabie Todd Swan 14 karat gold hand engraved overlay pen c1914

Mabie, Todd & Co. was established in 1860 in New York City and made gold nibs and pencils. Fountain pens made under the Swan name appeared by the late 1880s. Those early Mabie Todd eyedropper pens show some of the most elaborate and beautiful engraving work by any pen manufacturer and are thus prized by collectors. This Swan model, dated c1914, is a highly-detailed jeweler's hand engraved 14 karat gold cap and barrel overlay. All surfaces were polished and smoothed of any rough edge.

It's 5 ¼ inches long has Mabie Todd's 1904 patented Safety Screw Cap, which ensures no leakage when capped. The Blackbird nib and feed is a replacement, not original to the pen. The correct one would be a Mabie Todd Swan nib with a hard rubber overfeed.

Mabie Todd Blackbird Oriental Blue BB2/46 c1933

A Mabie Todd Blackbird Oriental Blue model BB2/46 from c1933. The Waterman Patrician uses the same vivid material as shown on the cap and barrel of this 5 ¼ inch long pen.

Oriental Blue Blackbirds do not appear in the 1927 to 1932 Mabie Todd catalogs, though the slim design model BB2 with no cap band and stepped clip Blackbird does. It's possible that this pen, model BB2 with color 46, Oriental Blue, first appeared in 1933.

Mabie Todd revamped their lines in 1934 to a more tapered and compact design with a quite different clip, and Blackbird pens followed suit. The Oriental Blue material continued to be used on the new redesigned model, probably from 1934 through at least the end of the 1930s.

Mabie Todd Blackbird Grey Silver Black Red Marble BB2/39 c1933

The Blackbird line was Mabie Todd's second tier below the Swan brand. Blackbird pens tended to be less ornate, with plainer nibs and clips and lacking trim, but still fitted with 14 karat gold nibs.

As with the top of the line Swan, Blackbirds had their name stamped in the same way on the nib, clip, section and barrel imprint, indicating that this model, while less expensive, was a quality Mabie Todd pen.

This model BB2 is an early 1930s pen, probably c1933, because it's not streamlined, as later Mabie Todds were. Most other brands followed Sheaffer's market leading Balance pen, introduced in 1929.

Mabie Todd color numbers followed the pen's model number and was stamped on the base of the barrel in the 1930s. This gray, silver, black, and red marble color is number 39, making this Blackbird a model BB2/39.

The Sacless Blackbird Fountpen BT200/82 Blue Gold and Black c1937-1940

The Sacless Blackbird Fountpen by Mabie Todd is a very uncommon and rare in the USA. This model BT200/82, made c1937-1940, is smaller at 4 ¾ inches long. Commonly called the Blackbird Topfiller, Mabie Todd named it the Sacless Blackbird Fountpen in their advertising. It has similarities to the larger Mabie Todd Visofil VT. Both are rubber sac plunger fillers with a visual ink reservoir in the barrel. The plunger mechanism is a spring wrapped with a sac that seals the end, and the sac acts as a diaphragm as the plunger is pumped, a similar operating principle as the Parker Vacumatic. The plunger itself is hidden under a long blind cap.

The Sacless Blackbird came in three colors, Black and Clear, Green Gold and Black, and this model, BT200/82, in Blue Gold and Black. They sold for seven shillings and sixpence in the United Kingdom. Matching pencils were available. When World War II broke out, the Mabie Todd Harlesdon Factory was destroyed, so repairs to these pens were done by replacing the plunger unit with a simple ink sac squeeze bulb.

The Sacless Blackbird Fountpen BT200/81 Green Gold and Black c1937-1940

This second Sacless Blackbird Fountpen is model BT200/81 in Green Gold and Black made c1937-1940.

Mabie Todd used Blackbird as the name for their second-tier, lower priced brand. They are marked with the Blackbird imprint and logo on the barrel, the Blackbird logo on the clip, and the Blackbird name on the nib stamping.

This cap and barrel celluloid appears to be unique to Mabie Todd and only used on these pens. The barrel imprint includes 'Blackbird' Self Filling Pen. Nothing in the imprint indicates the type of filler, as on the Mabie Todd Swan Visofil, which are marked "'Swan' Visofil Pen."

The Sacless Blackbird Fountpen BT200/60 Black and Clear c1937-1940

The BT200/60 Black and Clear is the third and final color of the Sacless Blackbird Fountpen by Mabie Todd.

The blind cap has been removed to show the plunger mechanism. The sac is a clear modern replacement to show the spring that surrounds the plunger. The angle of the shot and the background does not show the barrel transparency well, but it is a bit darker than the other two colors, a hint showing near the plunger. The clear barrels on these pens tend to amber. A non-ambered pen would be very rare.

When manufactured, c1937-1940, the plunger would have been inside a typical rubber sac and the mechanism would not show. Pens repaired during war time were done so with a simple rubber sac, changing the pen to a bulb squeeze filler.

Marukin hard rubber eyedropper filler c1920s

A very early Marukin hard rubber eyedropper filler dating to the 1920s. It features an unusual six sided clipless design, similar to the long body eyedroppers made earlier in the USA and UK.

Unlike many Japanese eyedropper pens that use an Onoto shut off plunger, this one is simple in design, filling by unscrewing the nib section from the barrel and dripping ink directly into the barrel using an eyedropper, thus the name. The cap is a slip-on friction fit type. The pen is 5 3/4 inches long with the cap on and 7 1/8 inches long with the cap posted on the end of the barrel. The ebonite is not urushi coated and shows color shades probably not existing when the pen was new. There is an interesting hobnail grip section at the barrel end. Featuring a 14 karat gold Marukin nib with gold filled trim marked K14. A very unusual older Japanese pen!

Marukin may have been a sub-brand of VANCO as the VANCO logo has been observed on clips of other Marukin pens. The VANCO logo is a V inside of a horizontal diamond. On cap bands it is next to the R14K stamp.

PenHero Quarterly
Marukin red hard rubber eyedropper pen with unusual two-piece cap c1930s

An interesting full size Marukin red hard rubber eyedropper pen which comes with an unusual two-piece cap. The top section of the cap, with the Warranted clip, can be removed by itself so one can hold the pen using the black ebonite part of the cap as a wide grip. The two cap pieces can also be removed as one unit, as the cap on a normal pen. It has a normal hard rubber section underneath made of the same ebonite as the pen barrel.

The Marukin nib is incredibly flexible and installed very deeply into the section so only the long tines show when the pen is opened. It's an eyedropper with a shut off valve which operates as many other Japanese eyedropper pens by slightly opening the end cap to allow ink flow to the section.

Morgan nib kamakura-bori Japanese art pen c1930s

This Japanese lever fill fountain pen features a Morgan nib, a premium nib maker from the 1930s. It features two complementing kamakura bori artwork designs on the front and back by an unknown pen maker. Kamakura-bori artwork is a technique in which many layers of urushi lacquer are layered onto the base pen, sometimes in several colors, and then carved to achieve the desired relief design.

The unusual two sided design is also two-toned. One side of the pen is the lighter six petal floral pattern and the other is a darker repeating hexagonal pattern. The design flows on the front and back in a wave rather than simply being two halves, a more difficult technique. Even the nib section has the flower design carved into it. The gold plated clip is unmarked and probably sourced from a parts company. It was common practice in Japan for small pen makers to obtain parts for pens from jobbers. The 14 karat gold Number 3 nib is stamped WARRANTED MORGAN PEN, not unexpected on custom and small maker pens. The pen is about 5 inches long capped.

Morison nib Parker 51 Aerometric copy c1950s

A similar design to a Parker 51 Aerometric, this pen features a Morison nib. Morison was established in 1918 in Gose, in the Nara prefecture. By 1953, the company was the leading pen manufacturer in Japan, with nearly 19 percent of the market. The formerly gold plated stainless steel Number 4 nib is stamped Morison Eternal and GOOD ARTICLE, a high-quality nib that may be a replacement.

The lack of makers marks on the pen or its squeeze filler unit is not uncommon with many Japanese pens. The body shape, squeeze filler, and the gold plated Parker 51 style Arrow clip indicate the influence of Parker designs in Japan. The clear pink acrylic barrel and cap is elaborately engraved, possibly by machine. The clear section is interesting, allowing one to view the ink level without opening the pen. Capped, the pen measures about 5 3/8 inches long.

Parker No. 60 Awanyu "Aztec" c1911-1916

The Parker No. 60 Awanyu "Aztec" pens were made from c1911-1916. In the August 1911 issue of Side Talks, the internal Parker Pen Company magazine, George S. Parker tells a story of how during the previous winter he traveled to Santa Fe, New Mexico, visited the museum of the Archeological Institute of America and saw, "the most wonderful collection of Indian and Aztec relics." During his tour of the museum, Parker saw what he was told was an Aztec design called, "Awanyu," which he was told was the, "Emblem of Mystic Power," "The preserver of life," and "the guardian of springs and streams." Parker obtained permission to copy the design and commissioned his jewelers to adapt it to a line of pens. This 6 ¼ inch No. 60 Awanyu "Aztec" in full 18 karat gold filled overlay that originally retailed for $20.00. Three other Aztec pens were made: No. 57 sterling silver half-overlay with cap crown, retailed for $10.00, No. 58 18 karat gold filled half-overlay with cap crown, retailed for $12.00, and No. 59 full sterling silver overlay, retailed for $16.00. The No. 59 is the most sought after and valuable pen today.

PenHero Quarterly
Parker Vacumatic Major Silver Pearl 1941

Parker began putting date codes on their pens, pencils and nibs in 1934, consisting of two digits, the first for the quarter and the second for the year. A pen marked "45" would be from quarter 4, 1935. In 1938, the code was changed where dots represent the quarter, three dots for the first quarter decreasing to zero dots for the fourth quarter. The code was found next to the barrel imprint and the system continued through 1948. Thus, this Vacumatic Major Silver Pearl was made in 1941. The pen has a date stamp of 1 next to the barrel imprint, indicating quarter four, 1941 and a 1 with a dot is stamped on the nib, indicating quarter 3, same year.

This pen has obvious wear and tear, but is interesting because of the two-tone platinum plated 14 karat gold Parker Arrow nib. Under the barrel end cap is the aluminum Speedline filler plunger, an improvement over the previous lock down plunger, which tended to break. Speedline pens have a longer blind cap than previous models. The 1941 Parker Vacumatic Major is about 5 ¼ inches long and came in Azure Blue Pearl, Laminated Jet, Golden Pearl, Silver Pearl, and Emerald Pearl, and sold for $8.75, with the matching pencil at $4.00.

Parker "VS" Blue c1947

Parker introduced the VS, or Vacumatic Successor, in 1946. This is an interesting mash-up of previous Parker designs. With the cap on, the pen has the outward appearance of a Parker 51 Vacumatic with a Lustraloy stainless steel cap, except that the clip is the tapered type, like those found on certain Parker Challenger and 1940s Duofold models. Pulling the cap off reveals a rather plain open nib, mated to a clear feed, like those found on inexpensive Wearevers. Removing the end cap reveals an aluminum filler button, not the expected plastic Vacumatic plunger.

The original 1946 colors, were black, grey, and rust, with blue following, probably the next year. The 5 1/2 inch long VS is simple to fill: remove the button cover, dunk the nib in ink, press the button and wait about 10-20 seconds for the ink sac to fill.

Parker 61 First Edition Heritage Cap in Green c1956

This Parker 61 has the 1956 First Edition Heritage Cap and the barrel and section is Caribbean Green. The original barrel and section for this pen was Rage Red, but since it had lost the gold Arrow inlaid piece in the nib section, it has been replaced. The First Edition shield, riveted to the lower front face of the cap, called out the newness of the 61 model. The 61 represented Parker's attempt to create the perfect filling system, a Teflon coated capillary capsule attached to the base of the nib section. It fills by putting the capsule end in the ink bottle and the perforated material inside the capsule absorbs and holds the ink. The Teflon coating keeps ink from sticking so the pen can be put back together without wiping.

This cap is the Heritage silver and yellow gold Rainbow cap, which polishes to a bright and shiny luster. There are three Rainbow caps. The other two are Heirloom (green and pink gold) and Legacy (nickel and silver). The pen is 5 3/8 inches long and came with Black, Grey Charcoal, Rage Red, Surf Green and Vista Blue sections and barrels and sold for $20.00.

Parker 41 Debutante c1957-1958

The Parker 41 is a less common variant of the Parker 51, introduced in 1956. The 41 was less expensive, offered with an octanium alloy nib, instead of gold, at price of $8.75 instead of the $12.50 starting price of the 51.

The Debutante is a special version of the 41 aimed at the fashion market, 5 ¼ inches long and offered at $6.00. The white painted cap has an engraved fish scale pattern with gold color fill. The Debutante was all about late 1950s colors and style. The pen came in Black, Coral, Grey, Turquoise, Pale Green, Pink and Aqua. The clip is the same design as the later Parker 45, which was introduced in 1960.

Parker 61 Presidential Waterdrop 9 karat gold c1966

The Parker Waterdrop guilloche pattern is a series of three straight engraved lines followed by a line that reminds of water drops running down a string.

This Parker 61 Presidential was made in the United Kingdom of 9 karat solid gold c1966. The Parker Hallmark shows clearly on the barrel, PPCo 9.375, the 9 karat gold mark. This model is 5 3/8 inches long and uses the 61 capillary filler unit. It also has an unusual double broad nib.

Presidential models were offered in the United Kingdom in both 9 and 18 karat versions. Known Presidential engraving patterns included Waterdrop (shown here), Fine Barley, Flamme, and Chevron, as well as an unengraved smooth version.

Parker 105 c1979-1982

The Parker 105 is an oddity, having an unusual high relief bark finish. There is also a new clip style and mounting. The matching ballpoint is a pull off cap type instead of the classic Parker push button type. Both pens are 5 1/8 inches long.

Parker introduced the 105 in 1979 and by 1982 it was discontinued. The first model was a rolled gold bark pattern that was later also offered in sterling silver. The rolled gold pen was used as the basis for the Prince Charles and Lady Diana wedding limited edition. Parker also made a smooth stainless steel Flighter version.

The 14 karat gold nib is like a long fingernail, extending straight from the end of the section and curving almost half way around. It gives the appearance that it might be a conical nib from the top. The clip is a chunky version of the classic Parker Arrow clip and is mounted on the face of the cap instead of using a washer type with a cap top screw similar to other Parkers.

Two Parker Big Red Duofolds, one c1928 and one c1992

Several years ago, the office of the U.S. Forces, Japan wanted a photo of a red Parker Duofold like the one General Douglas MacArthur used to sign the Japanese surrender documents on the battleship Missouri on September 2, 1945. The pen used by MacArthur was actually his wife's pen and has since been lost. The U.S. Forces, Japan team saw the photo of the c1928 Parker Duofold shown above (right) in an article on the Duofold and requested to have a copy of the shot.

This shot includes a modern red Duofold because Parker commemorated the event in 1995 with a Limited Edition Red Duofold Centennial with MacArthur's signature on the cap and an 18 karat gold cap top coin. Parker made 1,945 of those pens. MacArthur's wife was presented the number 1 Limited Edition in 1995 at the Waldorf Astoria Hotel in New York City. MacArthur's aide, who witnessed the signing, and MacArthur's wife both confirmed that the General used her Duofold as one of the signing pens. The left pen in the photo is the standard modern Red Duofold Centennial on which the Limited Edition was based.

Parker Duofold Greenwich special edition 1999

The Parker Duofold Greenwich was a 1999 special edition fountain pen and rollerball created to commemorate the new Millennium. It has an extraordinary guilloche engraved black resin cap and barrel. Named for the Royal Observatory in Greenwich, England, where traditionally at midnight each new day begins. Parker was the only pen company licensed to produce an official Greenwich pen, and use the Greenwich logo, to mark the Millennium celebration.

The Greenwich starts as a black Duofold Centennial that is machine engraved with a Fougere pattern on the cap and barrel. A special Greenwich emblem is set into the cap top. An extra wide single cap band is engraved "Parker Duofold Greenwich" in all caps. It has the two-tone Parker Arrow logo 18 karat gold Duofold nib and the original retail price was US $440.00.

PenHero Quarterly
Parker Duofold Centennial China 60th Anniversary 2009

The Parker Duofold Centennial China 60th Anniversary was a Limited Edition made for the Chinese market to commemorate the establishment of the People's Republic of China in 1949. The cap and barrel material is the Classic Pens diffusion bonded Flame Red and is shown with one of the rods from which they are turned.

The production pen has gold filled trim, including three cap bands. The special cap top emblem reads "China 1949-2009" with an image of the sun and a palace. The retail price was $1,600 each for the edition of 800 pens.

Platinum silver hand engraved leaf pattern pen c1950s

Platinum is one of the big three large pen companies in Japan. The company was founded by Shunichi Nakata in 1919 and the company name was changed to Platinum in 1928.

This sterling silver pen has a jeweler's hand engraved leaf pattern and dates from the 1950s. It has similar identifying attributes to contemporary Parker pens, which were popular in Japan, including a 14 karat gold Arrow nib, like the Vacumatic and the Arrow clip, like the 51. Platinum features their name prominently on both. Similar in size to the 5 ¼ inch long Parker 51.

The engraving work is deep and distinctive vine-like chains of four leaves each running parallel up the length of the cap and barrel. The engraving work appears to have been done by hand using a template as work varies from pen to pen, based on observations from several examples. The silver lever for the filling mechanism complements the silver cap and barrel. This is a rare and influential pen design and inspired the two copies that follow.

Japanese hand engraved silver leaf pattern pen c1950s

This Japanese hand engraved silver leaf pattern pen is an aerometric type filler made in the 1950s. The design is very similar to the rare Platinum silver lever-fill fountain pen shown previously. Similar in size and shape to 1950s Parker 51s and the clip is a direct copy of the 51 Arrow clip.

There are no maker's marks on this one, only the SILVER hallmark stamped on the cap lip. It's possible the pen was made by a jewelry shop emulating the Platinum design.

It has a clear section and has a King gold plated steel nib stamped 1952, possibly indicating the date, and pre-dating the JIS marks on pen nibs and the aerometric type filler would date this to the 1950s.

Japanese hand engraved gold plated leaf pattern pen c1950s

This Japanese hand engraved gold plated leaf pattern pen is a lever filler made in the 1950s and another copy of the Platinum silver leaf pattern pen. The maker is unknown and the pen has no hallmarking. It could be made of silver or another base metal.

The nib was made by Kabutogi Ginjiro, a famous nib maker of the mid-1950s. The nib is stamped STEADY and with JIS number 3233 indicating it is by Kabutogi Seisakusho, the company of Kabutogi Ginjiro. The SPECIAL stamped clip probably does not indicate the maker.

Popura kamakura bori eyedropper fountain pen c1930s

Popura (Popura Shugyo K.K.) was a small Tokyo based Japanese pen company and this eyedropper fountain pen dates from the early to mid c1930s. Both the gold plated clip and the 14 karat gold nib are stamped POPURA. The nib is also stamped TOKYO, NIPPON. The pen is standard size, about 5 1/4 inches long.

The cap and barrel carving represents Heian era coins using the kamakura bori technique. Urushi is applied in layers over an ebonite cap and barrel and the design is then cut into the finished pen. The Heian period was from 794 to 1185 and named after the ancient capital of Kyoto. Buddhism, Taoism and other Chinese influences flourished in Japan during this time.

Porsche Design P'3105 Pure Black fountain pen c2011-2017

The Porsche Design P'3105 Pure Black and Titanium fountain pens were announced January 2011, marking the beginning of Porsche Design's license partnership with Pelikan. The Pure Black was inspired by the Porsche Design black Chronograph I.

This is a very hefty pen, made of solid stainless steel including the milled clip, with all parts coated using the PVD process (physical vapor deposition) with a matte black coating of metal nitrides. The pen is delivered with a solid aluminum paperweight in the shape of a Porsche 911 car and is also matte black PVD coated.

The Pure Black line was made only as a fountain pen, 5 ½ inches long, offered with extra-fine, fine, medium and broad nibs, and retailing for $755. The line is now completely sold out.

Porsche Design Tec Flex Gold Special Edition 2015

The Porsche Design Tec Flex Gold Special Edition was released in October, 2015 as a short run special edition consisting only of a medium nib fountain pen, retailing for $1,250 and a matching ballpoint pen for $715.

It features a unique stainless steel mesh design made entirely of 24 karat gold plated stainless steel threads. This TecFlex design was meant to remind of the TecFlex braking hose material in high performance Porsche cars.

The cap and barrel ends are a matte 24 karat gold plated brass and the fountain pen features an 18 karat gold medium nib. The cap can snap onto the end of the barrel using the raised dots on the barrel end. It's 5 ¾ inches long.

Postal Reservoir Pen c1925-1928

The Postal Pen Company, Inc., of New York City was founded in the mid 1920s and manufactured the Postal Reservoir Pen. The company name reflects its marketing strategy, heavy advertising and only selling by mail order. Advertisements show the company was active at least from 1925 to 1928.

This is the larger size Postal Reservoir Pen, introduced probably in 1925, based on advertisements, and sold only by mail order for $2.50. They came in only two sizes, a larger model with a pocket clip for men and smaller one with a ringtop for women. The Postal Reservoir Pen is a bulb filler with a long breather tube that extends well into the clear celluloid barrel. Because the barrel is the ink reservoir, the pen holds a lot of ink.

The Postal Reservoir Pen is very large even by today's standards, being 5 11/16 inches long with the cap on and 6 15/16 inches long with the cap posted on the end of the barrel.

Recife Andy Warhol Mona Lisa Limited Edition 1996

Chaville, France based Recife (pronounced ray-seef) began making pens in 1987. The first pens established the principal design, a large cigar shaped swirled resin pen with a distinct clip and cap band design that echoes Waterman designs from the 1940s. The Andy Warhol Mona Lisa 1996 Limited Edition fountain pen is based on the Recife Mystique fountain and rollerball pen models. The Andy Warhol limited editions began with the 1994 Marilyn Monroe pen, followed by the Mona Lisa in 1996, and the Mao limited edition in 2001. The Mona Lisa was a 5,000 unit fountain and rollerball pen Limited Edition.

They are made from black and dark blue hand cast resin to match the coloring and tone of the 1978 Warhol Mona Lisa print. Hand turned on a lathe, each is a unique creation. Each has a silver plate clip and cap band, which is engraved with Andy Warhol's signature on the front and the Recife logo on the back. The pens are not individually numbered. They are fitted with an 18 karat gold two toned platinum masked open nib with Recife center stamped and framed with scrollwork. The pen is very large at 5 7/8 inches long capped and 6 7/8 inches long posted.

Sager Barrel of Ink Vacuum Pen c1926-1940

The clear Pyralin barrel of this Sager Vacuum Pen that holds the ink has heavily ambered over the years, but still has some transparency in bright light. It has a patented plunger filling mechanism which works with a single stroke where pulling out the plunger clears the ink reservoir in the barrel and pushing it in fills the pen. It's just under 5 inches long.

Solomon Sager founded the company in the 1920s and patented this filling mechanism in 1932. Originally called the Sager Vacuum Pen, at least through 1935, Sager later added the trademark Barrel of Ink, emphasizing the large capacity and that logo can be seen on the clip. Notable is the plated white metal nib. It may be an example of Sager's 1933 patent for a nib made of chrome plated Monel metal, more resistant than stainless steel to ink's corrosive effects. The Number 4 nib is stamped PROCESSED GUARANTEE NON-CORROSIVE and clearly has a silver color plating that is wearing off. They were offered by mail order for only $1 in 1935.

Sailor Profit sterling silver with a $5 gold coin epoxied to cap

An unusual Sailor Profit in sterling silver because it has a $5 gold coin epoxied to cap. Certainly, an oddity with a story behind it! The coin is epoxied at the base of the back of the cap, opposite the clip, and is about 5/8 across and bent to wrap around the cap. It is attached just above the "STERLING SILVER" stamping at the base the cap. The gold coin itself is marked LIBERTY and 1911 and has an Indian Chief head on it. It's not known why the coin is attached, but is not crisp like a factory job so it appears to be after purchase. Perhaps the owner wanted a coin to match the 1911 founding date of Sailor pen.

The cap band is stamped "SAILOR JAPAN FOUNDED 1911." It has a Sailor 14 karat gold nib. The pen is 5 1/2 inches long with the cap snapped on and 5 3/4 inches long posted.

Seishi Bosatsu kamakura-bori Japanese art pen c1930

Seishi Bosatsu is a protector deity of those born during the Year of the Horse and a provider of strength and wisdom. This Japanese eyedropper fountain pen is inscribed Seishi Bosatsu. There are two smaller characters on the bottom that may be the town where a temple dedicated to this bodhisattva is located. The creator of the pen is unknown, as with many small shop pen makers in Japan. Since 1930 was the Year of the Horse, the kamakura bori art work dates the pen to 1930 or near after.

The original Pawlonia wood box that came with the pen has the artist's seal and also reads Seishi Bosatsu on the top. Inside the cover of the box is name of artist and mark for "made by." The small label mentions "Year of The Horse." The gold-plated clip is marked CLIP, indicating a purchased part, the 14 karat gold Number 4 nib is stamped NEWEST POINTED SUPERIOR, and it is standard size, measuring five inches long closed.

Sheaffer Balance Autograph Ebonized Pearl Lever-fill c1934-1935

This Balance Autograph, the top of the line Ebonized Pearl model, with Sheaffer adding a 14 karat gold clip and 14 karat gold wide cap band to the largest Balance model, about 5 ¼ inches long.

The Autograph pen and pencil set sold for $30 in 1935, with $1 of the price being included for engraving the owner's signature on each instrument. The pen was offered in both lever and Vacuum-fil versions for the same price.

By the 1936 catalog, all versions of the Autograph pen are black only. This finish is sought after by collectors, especially in an Autograph model.

Sheaffer Balance Ebonized Pearl c1934-1935

Sheaffer claimed that the Ebonized Pearl material was made of genuine pearl inlaid into black radite. The material was introduced in 1934. Using real mother of pearl accounts for color variations on these pens. This example shows a green hue in the pearl chips. Sheaffer claimed that the pearl would never fade because the pearl chips are covered by a thin sheet of clear pyroxylin.

This is an earlier example, dated c1934-1935, because it lacks the Visulated section introduced on lever fill pens in the 1936 catalog. It's a model D3TC, about 5 5/16 inches long, which sold for $3.50. The nib is probably a later replacement because the correct nib would have a 3 on it.

Sheaffer Balance Jr. Ebonized Pearl c1937-1938

This is a later Sheaffer Balance Ebonized Pearl Junior, model D2V, with chrome plated trim. It's a smaller pen, about 4 7/16 inches long with the cap on. The D2V appears in the 1937 and 1938 catalog, the last year Ebonized Pearl was used.

Sheaffer literature indicates the unhallmarked Junior nib is solid gold, probably 12 karat. The pen sold for $2.75 and was also available as a Vacuum-fil pen.

Sheaffer Crest Masterpiece Vacuum-fil c1942-1944

Sheaffer announced the Triumph Lifetime line to its dealers on January 1, 1942 and first advertised the line in Life Magazine on July 27. The line featured Sheaffer's new and innovative conical Triumph "Sheath-Point" nib.

The Sheaffer Crest Masterpiece is a combination of the 14 karat gold Triumph Masterpiece cap and a standard Triumph Crest barrel and nib section. Note the White Dot on the end of the barrel. It would be several years before Sheaffer developed the procedure to mount the dot on a metal cap.

The cap and clip are hallmarked 14K. Without a 1942-1944 price list, the actual price is unknown, but the previous model 1941 pen sold for $35.00 and by 1946, the following Triumph II model pen sold for $50.00.

Sheaffer Tuckaway Vacuum-fil Autograph pen and pencil set c1946-1947

The full name of this 4 7/16 inch long pen was the 'Triumph Tuckaway For Your Autograph.' These pens are notable for their short duck bill clips. Previous Tuckaway models were clipless. The cap and barrel are made of Black Radite and the clip and 9/16 inch cap band are hallmarked 14K. The cone tip of the pencil is also hallmarked 14K. It has a solid 14 karat gold Triumph nib.

Made in both lever and vacuum-fil versions the pen sold for $20 and the matching pencil was $15. Vacuum-fil pens filled by unscrewing the barrel end cap and pulling out the long plunger. Dipping the nib in ink, the pen is filled by a single quick downstroke of the plunger. Because the ink fills the barrel, these small pens can hold a surprisingly large amount of ink. Autograph Tuckaways are probably the most difficult black Sheaffer Autograph pens to obtain.

Sheaffer Snorkel Demonstrator c1952-1959

Sheaffer Snorkel Demonstrators are generally dated from c1952-1959. The pens were produced for dealers to demonstrate the inner workings of the new Snorkel filling system. Most were probably made at the beginning of Snorkel production though it's possible Sheaffer made some over the life of the pen line.

This demonstrator has a Triumph 14 karat two-tone 14 karat gold nib with platinum mask, clear plastic cap and barrel, gold-filled clip and 3/8" wide gold-filled cap band. It's essentially a clear plastic Valiant.

These were not marketed for sale and produced only in clear plastic. Some demonstrators can be found with regular production caps, probably replacements. Many demonstrators have cracked plastic, possibly because the clear plastic is less able to deal with stress, and the clip spring would be a pressure point that if broken, a cap swap would be an easy solution.

Sheaffer Snorkel Masterpiece c1952-1959

The Sheaffer Snorkel Masterpiece c1952-1959 is a rare find. The Masterpiece was the top of the line Sheaffer Snorkel, with the cap, clip, barrel, and end cap all hallmarked solid 14 karat gold. The Triumph "Lifetime" 14 karat two-tone gold nib, plated with platinum, was unique to this model Snorkel.

These were pricey pens, retailing for $110.00 in 1958. Sheaffer also made this pen in the United Kingdom in 18 karat and 9 karat gold hallmarked models with a fine barley machine engraved cap and barrel.

The Snorkel pen is a Touchdown filler with a narrow tube that extends through the feed to allow filling without immersing the nib in ink. The Snorkel tube extends as the barrel end cap is unscrewed to pull out the plunger. Pneumatic air pressure in the down stroke of the cylindrical plunger compresses the sac inside a cylinder in the barrel and fills the pen. The only thing that gets inky is the Snorkel tube, which retracts back into the section, underneath the nib, after filling.

Sheaffer Snorkel Sentinel Mandarin Orange 1956-1959

One of the more difficult Snorkel colors to find, Mandarin Orange is one of the new Snorkel colors introduced in 1956. Mandarin Orange pens have black sections. The color was used only on White Dot Snorkel pens: the Statesman, Clipper, Valiant, and Sentinel models. The Sentinel, shown here, has a polished stainless steel cap with gold filled trim and sold for $22.50 in 1956 and the matching pencil was $7.50. The "Ensemble" pen and pencil set sold for $30.00 in 1956. Snorkel pens are 5 9/16 inches long.

Sheaffer PFM I c1959-1963

By 1959, Sheaffer was leading the market in pen sales with its successful Snorkel line. The 1950s saw Sheaffer and others move away from the larger and fatter pens of previous decades with a shift to more slender pens. The new PFM, or Pen For Men, introduced in 1959, was return to larger pens intended for larger hands.

The PFM was Sheaffer's last and largest Snorkel model, introduced at a price range of $10 for the all plastic and stainless trimmed PFM I to $25 for the gold filled cap and trim PFM V. Like another now highly collectible pen, the Parker Duofold Mandarin, the PFM was not a great success, with the line being pared of models later in the production run. The PFM full line was made through 1963, when Sheaffer introduced the Lifetime cartridge pens.

The Sheaffer PFM I is the base pen of the PFM line. It has a solid color plastic cap and barrel, a polished stainless steel clip and cap band, and a palladium silver nib. The PFM I is the only model without the White Dot. These pens sold for $10 and the matching pencil was $4.95. PFMs were produced in black, blue, burgundy, green, and gray.

Sheaffer PFM II c1959-1963

The Sheaffer PFM II is the second pen of the Pen For Men line. It has a frosted finish stainless steel cap and a solid color plastic barrel and nib section. The clip is polished steel and has the Sheaffer White Dot at the top. The Inlaid nib is made of palladium silver alloy. The 5 ¼ inch long pen sold for $12.50 and the matching pencil was $5.

The pen uses the same Snorkel filling system as the Snorkel pens and it operates in the same way. Sheaffer offered the PFM with eight nib choices: accountant, extra fine, fine, reporter, medium fine, medium, broad, and stub.

Sheaffer PFM III c1959-1963

The Sheaffer PFM III is the higher trim version of the PFM I, also having a solid color injection molded plastic cap, barrel and nib section. The clip and trim are gold filled, and the clip has the Sheaffer White Dot at the top. The large Inlaid nib is 14 karat gold.

The cap band on plastic cap PFM pens have a strong taper downward toward the barrel. Sheaffer used the Inlaid nib as a symbol for this pen and other Inlaid nib pens such as the Sheaffer Compact and Imperial models. It appears as a logo on the PFM gift box.

Sheaffer PFM IV c1959-1963

The Sheaffer PFM IV has a polished stainless steel cap and plastic barrel. The clip, cap band, trim and plunger end cap are gold filled and the clip has the Sheaffer White Dot at the top. The large Inlaid nib is 14 karat gold.

Pictured showing the Snorkel tube extended from the section under the nib and the plunger pulled out from the barrel. The pen fills by unscrewing the end cap from the barrel, which extends the Snorkel, then pulling out the plunger, then dipping only the Snorkel into the ink bottle and finally quickly pushing in the plunger, which pneumatically compresses an ink sac inside the barrel, filling the pen. Screwing in the end cap retracts the plunger and it is ready to write with no wiping. An incredibly complex pen that works as advertised!

Sheaffer PFM V c1959-1963

The Sheaffer PFM V is the black tie model of the Pen For Men line. The PFM V has an interrupted linear engraved gold filled cap and plastic barrel, gold filled clip and plunger cap end plate, and a 14 karat gold Inlaid nib. The pen came in all of the PFM colors but shows its formal side in black and gold. The pen was a pricey $25 when new, with the matching pencil $10 additional.

Sheaffer PFM V c1959-1963, the two cap types

Detail showing the two types of PFM V caps. Though at first glance the cap shells and clip appear to be the same on both versions, each has a distinctly different engraved lines design. Both caps have four long and four shorter sets of parallel engraved lines. The shorter sets align with the clip.

The right cap matches the illustration in the 1962 Sheaffer repair manual where the design's longer sets of engraved lines are even at the top. On this first cap version, the shorter sets of engraved lines are much shorter than on the later cap and they start about 1/8 inch higher from the cap lip than sets of long lines.

The second cap version, shown on the left, has a pair of engraved lines that extend out from the middle of the longer set even with the White Dot on the clip. These lines are visible looking at the front face of the cap. There are examples of the second cap design not marked with the Sheaffer logo.

PenHero Quarterly
Sheaffer Lifetime 2000 c1963-1964

Sheaffer introduced the Lifetime cartridge pen line in 1963 to mark the company's 50th anniversary. Lifetime pens came with a lifetime guarantee certificate for the registered owner. The new line, which ran through 1964, was composed of cartridge versions of many of the prior year Imperials. Sheaffer marked them Lifetime on the clip, the 14 karat gold nib, and in the plastic above the cap band.

The Lifetime 2000 was the last Sheaffer Autograph, though not so named. Sheaffer Autographs featured 14 karat gold cap bands and the Autograph name meant that the band was intended for the owner's signature. Earlier versions also included a 14 karat gold clip, not present on the 2000.

The 2000, about 5 3/8 inches long, was available only with a black plastic cap and barrel and sold for $20.00. A matching pencil was available for $12.50.

Sheaffer Legacy with Demonstrator nib section c1995

This Sheaffer Legacy has a demonstrator nib section, made for the first version of the Legacy, introduced in 1995. Legacy demonstrator sections are rare and were not released to dealers. After the closing of the Sheaffer factory in Fort Madison, Iowa, parts from the design shop started to trickle out into the market, including prototype pens.

This section is not glued together or sealed like the section on a finished Legacy. It shows the ample room for a long feed with very wide fins. This makes it clear why Sheaffer Legacy nibs write as wet and evenly as they do. The tabs that secure the nib in place when it is molded into the section can also be seen.

The Legacy is 5 3/8 inches long and uses a modified Touchdown pneumatic filling system. Sheaffer introduced this filling system in 1949. To operate, the user unscrews the end cap of the pen to pull out the cylindrical plunger. Air pressure in the down stroke of the plunger compresses the sac inside the cylinder and fills the pen. The ink sac is contained in a gold plated converter that can be removed by unscrewing the nib section so cartridges can be used.

Sheaffer Balance Limited Edition 1997

Sheaffer introduced the Balance Limited Edition in 1997 and followed with the new cartridge/converter Balance II line in 1998. This oversize Limited Edition lever fill pen, about 5 ½ inches long, was made as an homage to the Sheaffer Balance pens of the 1930s.

The Balance Limited Edition was 6000 pieces and a small number of lever fill clear demonstrators were also made. The Limited Edition's acrylic is a marbling of celadon green, vermilion and black. The nib is a replica of an early two-tone palladium plated Sheaffer Lifetime nib done in 18 karat gold and medium grade. The clip is stamped with the Sheaffer's style logo and all trim is 22 karat gold electroplated. Each has its edition number stamped on the barrel.

Sheaffer introduced its new Balance II cartridge / converter pen line in 1998, featuring beautiful marbled acrylics as well as solid colors.

Sheaffer Prelude Persimmon prototype color pen c2000s

A Sheaffer Prelude prototype color pen that was probably intended as part of the varsity college book store and imprint market. Sheaffer made lots of Preludes specifically to be printed or engraved for the promotional market. Many were lacquered in one of the primary colors of major universities for their bookstores.

A persimmon color, this was likely intended for that market, but was never produced and only a few were made. When the Sheaffer factory in Fort Madison, Iowa closed, several of these pens were given out as gifts. Always interesting to find an unusual variation or prototype of a mass produced popular pen like the Prelude!

The Sheaffer Prelude, a 5 3/16 inch long pen, was introduced in 1997 and the latest models were released in 2016. Most Prelude fountain pens have stainless steel nibs with various stamped designs, some with two-tone gold plating as on this example. Some Prelude Signature models for the Asia markets were offered with 14 karat gold nibs.

Swan Japan Daruma (Bodhidharma) carved pen c1935-1938

The carved image of Daruma, as he is known in Japan, is the Indian monk Bodhidharma, who is believed to have brought Chan Buddhism to China in the 5th or 6th century. The image is carved into the surface of the pen and then painted with colored urushi lacquer. His face is orange and his robe is red and green.

The clip has the Swan Japan logo at the top and SWAN is carved in the barrel just below the image. The owner's name, Iida, is also on the barrel. The pen is about 5 inches long and has a 14 karat gold PERFECT number 4 nib. The gold nib dates the pen to pre-war, c1935-1938. Swan was founded in 1900 and was using the trade name for pens before Mabie Todd began exporting to Japan.

Steady nib Japanese flat top eyedropper pen c1920s

A silver flat top Japanese eyedropper pen made probably before World War II. There is a simple floral design engraved on the cap and barrel and the pen is stamped SILVER on the cap top. There are no maker's marks, but the pen was likely made by a jeweler or possibly by VANCO, based on similar pens VANCO made.

The 5 1/16 inch long pen has a post war JIS marked nib. Many Japanese pre-war pens had gold nibs, but by 1937 gold was a restricted from commercial use in Japan and pen nibs in many cases were sold for the gold content and replaced with stainless steel nibs. Nibs may also have been replaced after World War II when gold nibs became available again.

The Japanese Industrial Standards (JIS) for nibs were established in 1954 and nibs would be marked with the JIS symbol and in many cases a number. STEADY was the trademark used by Kabutogi Ginjiro, considered the best nib maker of the era.

PenHero Quarterly
Tuckersharpe Ink Master c1950s

The Tuckersharpe Pen Company was founded in 1952 by Percy Tucker in Richmond, Virginia. He used himself as the spokesman in some of his company's advertising. The company made inexpensive fountain and ballpoint pens claiming millions of sales.

The Ink Master exemplifies Tuckersharpe lever-fill fountain pen design features, including a clear section, clear feed, pull off cap, and a removable Esterbrook type nib unit. Tuckersharpe borrowed ideas from other pen makers. The removable Esterbrook type nib unit will swap with an Esterbrook made section. Tuckersharpe used the "Wing Flow" name for the nib, which had nothing to do with the nib design of the same name by the Chilton Pen Company, which had tabs that wrap around the feed to hold the nib securely in place. Most obvious is the company name, a play on Eversharp.

The Ink Master is 5 ¼ inches long and sold for 49 cents. It came in black, navy blue, light blue, green, red and white.

Uetosi eyedropper fountain pen with S.S.S. nib c1940s

Uetosi was one of the many small pen makers in Japan that made their own caps and barrels and then bought needed hardware from larger pen makers or parts shops. The barrel imprint on this pen is UETOSI & CO., with a logo to the left and kanji characters below. It's a large pen at 5 3/16 inches long.

The clip is marked STEN and is like many generic clips made by small metal shops and may be the maker's mark. The trim appears to be chrome plated and the cap and barrel appears to be black resin.

The pen has a medium S.S.S. nib, made by San Esu, a smaller pen maker in business from 1911 to the 1960s. S.S.S. made gold nibs, but during World War II gold was a wartime resource and pen nibs in Japan were made using stainless steel.

PenHero Quarterly
Wahl Eversharp Coronet c1936-1941

The Wahl Eversharp Coronet c1936-1941 is widely considered to be the most art deco pen ever made. Announced in 1936 in an ad with the headline "Gold is back!" the Coronet was the finest pen in the Eversharp lineup, selling for $10.00, with a $1.00 premium for an adjustable point nib, which has a large slider on top. This one has the standard nib. The pen featured Eversharp's Safety Ink Shut-Off system and this one is complete with the shut off tab under the nib section.

The full gold filled engine turned cap and barrel pen came in two versions, having either black or red Pyralin celluloid showing in the triangular shaped cutouts on the cap and barrel and as a large square cap top piece. The red Pyralin on this 5 1/16 inch long example is marbled. The barrel end face is stamped EVERSHARP across the center with GOLD FILLED and MADE IN USA curved above and below.

Wahl Eversharp Coronet Gold and Green Shell Pyralin c1936-1941

This Wahl Eversharp Coronet Gold and Green Shell Pyralin is one of the three types of Eversharp Coronet pens with plastic barrels. The Wahl Eversharp Coronet Gold and Green Shell Pyralin, model 17734, sold for $10.00 and the matching pencil, model 10604, for $5.00. The plastic barrel models of these 5 1/16 inch long Coronets are also distinguished from the full cap and barrel gold filled model by the two rows of rectangular windows in the cap, but also have the same square faceted Pyralin cap top jewel.

Because the clear ink view section was disintegrating, this pen was sent for repair. The section replacement was nicely done and only shows under careful examination. The cap shows typical usage wear.

The two other plastic barrel models feature a black barrel, with a choice of rhodium plated cap (pen $8.75 and pencil $2.75) or gold filled cap (pen $10.00 and pencil $5.00). The cap design is identical to the pen shown.

PenHero Quarterly
Eversharp Symphony 1st Generation c1948

The Eversharp Symphony was designed by Paris, France born industrial designer Raymond Loewy (1893-1986). Loewy emigrated to the United States in 1919 and started his own design company in 1927. Loewy designed numerous consumer goods, emphasizing streamlining and modern materials. Eversharp had high hopes that engaging this famous designer would help recreate the magic and success of the Dreyfuss-designed Skyline.

The first year Symphony pens are notable for the original Loewy design of the "slipper" cap, where the cap has slightly offset halves, with a pronounced "step" edge at the top. If viewed from the side, the bottom half of the cap (opposite from the clip) extends farther than the top half, giving it the distinctive asymmetrical "slipper" look. These 1st Generation pens are the only ones with a metal thread ring in the section and "EVERSHARP SYMPHONY" and "MADE IN U.S.A." stamped just below. The clip face is angled and there is no cap band. The nib and feed is essentially the same as in the previous Skyline pens. Barrel colors were black, blue, green, and red. The fountain pen, model 500, 5 7/16 inches long, sold for $5.00, and the matching Repeater pencil, model 1500, sold for $3.75.

Eversharp Golden Symphony, 2nd Generation c1949-1950

An Eversharp Golden Symphony, a 2nd Generation model, catalog number 705 with a Dubonnet (burgundy) barrel. These pens were made c1949-1950. The Golden Symphony has a gold filled cap and clip and sold for $12.75. They came in Black, Blue, Brown, Dubonnet, and Green, darker colors than the 1st Generation pens. The bright red of the original pens was replaced with a darker burgundy, for example. They are also a little longer at 5 ½ inches. The matching Repeater pencil sold for $6.00.

The primary differences in the 2nd generation pen from the original Loewy design were a softening of the edges of the cap to a more rounded design, finishing the cap in a high polish, flattening the clip face, adding the words "Made in USA" to the clip top, and simplifying the section, leaving out the stamping. Eversharp added trim rings and gold plate to the cap finishes, creating a lineup of six total models. The pencil gained a small ring engraving in the cone tip.

Eversharp Symphony, 3rd Generation with brushed steel cap, c1951-1952

An interesting version of the Eversharp Symphony, a 3rd Generation pen with a brushed steel cap, made c1951-1952. Eversharp dropped the Loewy "slipper" cap design in 1951 in favor of a streamlined "bullet" cap. This last version loses the distinctive look of the Symphony and follows blunt or cigar shape design cues from other brands, such as the Sheaffer models of the late 1940s. It is likely, due to Eversharp's deteriorating financial position, this simplification was a cost cutting move.

The 3rd Generation Symphony maintained the same length, model numbers, and price points as the 2nd Generation line, but they were no longer called Symphony in Eversharp advertising. There is a brushed steel cap 2nd Generation Symphony, so this model, as others, is a carry over. The standard model 701 Symphony fountain pen sold for $5.00, so this pen either sold for the same or less. The late Symphony models came in Black, Blue, Burgundy, and Green. An interesting design tidbit: The chrome plated cap band is a sleeve insert that fits onto the base of the cap. Probably easier to plate the piece and attach it to the rest of the cap.

Waterford Marquis Arista Prism Purple c2005-2007

The Marquis by Waterford Arista Prism Purple fountain pen cap, barrel, and section was machine turned from a striking swirled purple and white resin and accented with highly polished chrome plated trim. The Arista Prism line came in mocha, caramel, and rainbow color resin.

Each pen has a Schmidt stainless steel nib, and most nibs were stamped "Iridium Tip Germany." Some nibs included the Schmidt logo. The pen uses international type ink cartridges or a converter.

A very light weight pen, but full size, at 5 1/4 inches long. The fountain pen retailed for $75. Matching rollerball ($60) and ballpoint ($50) pens were also made. The line was discontinued and closed out in 2008.

PenHero Quarterly
Waterman Corinth c1950-1951

Waterman introduced the Corinth model in 1948, a pen with an Astralite cap, Waterman's name for a polished stainless steel cap, and enhanced with a gold plated clip and trim. This first Corinth had radial lines engraved in the cap starting below the clip and extending above the cap lip, with no engraving between the clip and an engraved star at the cap lip. Waterman updated the Corinth Astralite cap in late 1948 with a new engraving pattern of longitudinal pairs of parallel lines with two pairs of ring engravings forming a cap band near the cap lip.

This version of the Waterman Corinth was a short lived model, advertisements show 1950-1951, and known as the Executive in Canada. Its narrow cap band distinguishes it from the next Corinth model. The Corinth, a 5 ¼ inch long pen, was sold in both standard and Taperite versions in red, blue, grey and black for $11.50, and with a matching "Selfeed Metermatic" pencil for $16.50. Sets came in a Royal Blue display box. The cap tops allowed the owner to tell which instrument they were using by touch, with a rounded fountain pen cap top and a concave pencil cap top. Waterman had an earned reputation for excellent nibs and touted that its pen points were hand ground.

Waterman Man 100 Gold "Specimen" c1988-2004

The Waterman Man 100 Gold "Specimen" c1988-2004 is basically a faux gold plated version of the solid gold MAN 100. The pen enabled dealers to be able to safely demonstrate the over $10,000 pen without having them showing handling marks. A wealthy customer could try this pen out and get a sense of what they were buying and know when they ordered the real pen they would be getting one that is untouched.

The full 18 karat solid gold model is a heavily fluted Godron design, first offered in 1988. The same design was also available in solid sterling silver and as a twist action ballpoint. All elements of the 5 5/8 inch long solid gold pen would be hallmarked, including the cap, section, barrel, end cap and clip. This pen is stamped "SPECIMEN" on the cap, barrel and section to make sure there is no doubt that this one is a facsimile gold plated demonstrator.

PenHero Quarterly
Wearever Pacemaker c1954-1960

A lesser known Wearever pen with a better known Wearever name, the c1954-1960 Pacemaker in blue. There exists counter top ephemera, trademark information and packaging that confirms the name and features of this late and possibly last use of the Wearever Pacemaker name on a fountain pen.

Some examples of these pens have a barrel imprint that has the Pacemaker name. The pen features "Replace-A-Point" nib / feed units, trademarked January 31, 1954, that unscrew, similar to an Esterbrook pen, and offered in extra fine, flexible fine, medium flexible, medium firm, broad and steno. The stainless steel nib does away with the silly overfeed of the Pennant, but retains the C-flow clear feed. Notable higher quality differences from other Wearever pens include an all metal cap in what looks like brushed steel topped with a metal cap top and a metal trim ring that actually closes flush when the cap is screwed on. These Pacemakers were 5 3/8 inches long and based on known examples were offered in red, blue, gray and green. They sold for $1.95.

Wearever squeeze filler fountain pen c1955-1957

This is a previously unknown Wearever squeeze filler fountain pen in navy blue. Removing the cap reveals a squeeze filler! There is no evidence of a breather tube, so it's probably not an aerometric type. There is a simpler "press bar" version of a squeeze filler on the early 1950s Wearever Supreme and 1951 Wearever Triboro gold bullet shaped pen. The unit is a long cylindrical cage around a rubber ink sac with a cut out for a press bar, very similar to the design used by Eversharp in the 1953 to 1957 Slim Ventura. This Wearever filling unit is more refined and looks a lot like the filling unit on the Parker 51 Special, launched in 1950. The 51 Special has the same simple design with the ply-glass reservoir covered by a U shaped metal bar. This unit looks like a copy. It is a combination of design elements from other Wearever pens. The cap and clip is similar to the 2nd generation Pennant, c1957-1960, with its coin edge plastic cap lip that matches the barrel color and the flat faced chrome plated clip, however the navy blue barrel color is like the colors of the early 1950s Pennants. The barrel, with its metal end cap is similar to the design of the Wearever Cartridge Pen c1957-1960. The metal cap top jewel is identical to the last version of the Pacemaker c1957-1960. This one probably dates to c1955-1957. It's 5 7/16 inches long.

Wearever Lady Fair shell pink cartridge pen, mesh pattern c1958-1960

A Wearever Lady Fair shell pink cartridge pen, engraved with a mesh pattern. Even in mint condition, it's easy to see that these were mass produced. Otherwise, these are actually pretty well made.

Like other 1950s Wearever pens, the Lady Fair uses Wearever's C-flow clear feed, a feature that allowed the user to check the ink level in the pen without opening it to look at the cartridge.

The clipless Lady Fair is 5 1/8 inches long. They sold new for $1.95 with two cartridges and a holder. A package of six replacement cartridges sold for 49 cents.

Shown is the boxed set that included a pen holder with two spare cartridges. A set with matching pencil was also offered.

Wearever Lady Fair shell pink cartridge pen, wave pattern c1958-1960

A Wearever Lady Fair shell pink cartridge pen, engraved with a wave pattern. These are brass base metal pens that with engraved patterns that are painted and then the engraving is filled with gold paint. On many examples, even mint pens like this one, the gold is not perfectly applied as can be easily seen on this one.

Wearever offered these pens in three engraved patterns, a mesh pattern, a short wave pattern and a long wave pattern. This is the shorter wave pattern.

The stainless steel nib is similar to the nib on the Pennant and Pacemaker and was offered in extra fine, flexible fine, medium flexible, medium firm, broad and steno.

PenHero Quarterly
Wearever Lady Fair plum cartridge pen, mesh pattern c1958-1960

This Wearever Lady Fair cartridge pen is in plum and engraved with the mesh pattern.

The Wearever Lady Fair cartridge pen was inspired by the Lady Sheaffer Skripsert Cartridge Fountain Pen introduced in 1958. David Kahn, Inc., the company behind Wearever, launched this similar looking ink cartridge pen line the same year.

The Lady Fair was made in five of the fashion colors of the late 1950s, black, plum, harvest, aqua or shell pink.

Well eyedropper fountain pen with Sailor nib c1940s

A Well eyedropper pen is made with an unusual deeply cut ribbed design on a grey marble resin. The pen barrel is stamped WELL, with a logo to the left and FOUNTAIN PEN below.

Well pens were made by Mitsumoto-Honten and distributed by Diamond. The company was a smaller pen maker from the 1920s through the 1950s.

The pen has a very long tine Number 5 Sailor stainless steel nib, a sign of mid to late 1940s pens. It's 5 1/8 inches long and quite light. The eyedropper shut off is opened slightly.

Yotsubishi kawari-nuri sakura (cherry) bark pattern pen c1955-1959

This Yotsubishi fountain pen is decorated in a free pattern, or Kawari-nuri, to simulate sakura (cherry) bark. The design dates the pen to c1955-1959. The cap, barrel and nib section are all urushi coated and then worked to the pattern shown. Japanese cherry tree bark has a distinctive pattern and it can be seen featured in wooden objects, such as boxes, frames, and vases. The free form artwork is intended to recreate the pattern with the red urushi lacquer base and contrasting elements.

Ishi-Shoten, also known as Ishi & Co., was established in Tokyo in 1925 by pen maker Yoshinosuke Ishii. Following the lead of Pilot, which began making maki-e pens in the 1920s, Ishi-Shoten, though a small company with initially as few as ten workers, began competing by making inexpensive maki-e pens. Ishi-Shoten used the four diamond trademark, yotsubishi in Japanese, and the mark can be found on the clip top. In reference materials, on the pens, and in catalogs, there are three spellings, Yotsubishi, Yotubisi, and Yotubishi. The company ceased operations in 1984. The pen has a squeeze filler, similar to a Parker 51 aerometric bark in operation and is about 5 ¼ inches long.

Manufacturers

Aikin Lambert - Aikin Lambert was founded in New York City to make gold pen nibs sometime after the Civil War. The company began to make fountain pens in the 1880s.

Aurora - Aurora is Italy's largest pen maker and was founded in Turin in 1919. The company has a long history of manufacturing very high quality pens, beginning, as many early twentieth century pen companies, with hard rubber and overlay eye dropper, safety, and lever fill pens.

Classic Pens / Lambrou Pens - Classic Pens Limited was formed in England in 1987. Fountain pens were a shared passion for the two founders, Andreas Lambrou and Keith G. Brown. This culminated in 1990 with the launch of the Classic Pens CP collection of limited editions. The company is noted for its limited edition pens in sterling silver and maki-e, based both on the flagship pens of leading pen companies. The company is now named Lambrou Pens.

Cleo Skribent - Herbert Wurach founded Herbert Wurach Precision Engineering in 1945 as a manufacturer and supplier of metal parts used to manufacture writing instruments and its own ballpoint pen. The successful Skribent, introduced in 1965, an "Inkpen with a tubular nib in 8 different widths," marketed to technical draftsmen and designers, made Cleo the leading manufacturer of pens in the socialist world.

Conklin - Roy Conklin invented the crescent filling system, a press bar system with a curved ridge that squeezed an ink sac in the barrel, in 1898 and founded what became the Conklin Pen Company in Toledo, Ohio. The company is famous for innovation, including the piston filling Nozac pen.

Crocker - The Crocker Pen Company was founded in 1902 in Boston, Massachusetts, by Seth Sears Crocker, and later moved to New York City. Crocker is noted for interesting designs, particularly for its Ink-Tite blow filler pens, patented in 1901 and 1904.

Giuliano Mazzuoli - Italian designer Giuliano Mazzuoli manufactures writing instruments in Firenze, Italy. His designs are inspired by everyday objects such as the Moka coffee maker, mechanical tools and racing.

Ikoma - Ikoma was a famous jewelry shop in Osaka. Founded in 1870 by Gonkichi Ikoma as a jewelry and watch workshop, G. Ikoma Ltd. was established in 1923 and moved into the landmark Ikoma Building in 1930.

Mabie Todd - Mabie, Todd & Company was formed in New York City in 1860, as a partnership between John Mabie and Edward Todd. The company made many ornate and beautiful writing instruments, including gold pens, which would today be called nibs, early patent pencils, dip pen holders, and pencil cases.

Marukin - Marukin was a Japanese maker of high-end fountain pens in the 1930s. Marukin may have been part of Marukin Shoyu Co., a food maker of one of the top five soy sauce brands in Japan, based on Shodo Island.

Morgan – Little is known about the Morgan pen company of Japan, a nib maker in business in the 1930s.

Morison - Morison was established in 1918 in Gose, in the Nara prefecture of Japan. By 1953, the company was the leading pen manufacturer in Japan, with nearly 19 percent of the market.

Parker - The Parker pen company was established by George Safford Parker in 1888 and its first fountain pen was patented in 1889. The company was highly innovative, both technically and with innovative design. The Lucky Curve feed was patented in 1894. The Duofold fountain pen was introduced in 1921, and the red models became known as the 'Big Red.' The groundbreaking Parker 51 was introduced in 1939 with its innovative hooded nib, a design that changed the direction of the industry.

Platinum - One of the big three pen makers in Japan, the company was founded by Shunichi Nakata in 1919. The company name was changed to Platinum in 1928. Platinum's flagship #3776 model was launched in 1978. The name comes from the height in meters of Mount Fuji, the tallest and most symbolic mountain in Japan. The President line was launched in 1994 and the Izumo in 2010.

Popura - Popura (Popura Shugyo K.K.) was a small Tokyo based Japanese pen company and this eyedropper fountain pen dates from the early to mid c1930s.

Porsche Design Group - Founded in 2003 as a subsidiary of Porsche AG to create designer accessories and licensing products under the Porsche brand.

Postal - The Postal Pen Company, Inc., of New York City was founded in the mid 1920s and manufactured the Postal Reservoir Pen. The company name reflects its marketing strategy, heavy advertising and only selling by mail order. Advertisements show the company was active at least from 1925 to 1928

Manufacturers

Recife – Recife began in Paris, France in 1930 as a leather goods company. Fine pens were added in 1987, with a focus on distinctive materials and designs.

Sager - Solomon M. Sager started the Sager Pen Corporation at least as early as November 1, 1926. Sager was an innovator, introducing improvements to vacuum fill and ink pellet pens. Trademark registrations listed the company's address as 36 South State Street, Chicago, Illinois.

Sailor – The story by Sailor, Japan is that its founder, Kyugoro Sakata, an engineer from Hiroshima, Japan, was shown a fountain pen by a British sailor in 1911, thus the founding date of the company and the origin of the name. Based in Hiroshima, Japan, Sailor is one of the big three Japanese pen makers.

Sheaffer - The Sheaffer pen company was founded by Walter A. Sheaffer in Fort Madison, Iowa in 1913 and introduced its lever-filling fountain pen that same year. In 1924, Sheaffer became the first pen company to mass-produce plastic pens, giving the cellulose nitrate plastic developed by DuPont the trade name "Radite." The resulting Jade green pens became best sellers. Sheaffer was an innovator, as seen in its conical Triumph nib in the early 1940s, the 1952-1959 Snorkel pen, with the most complex filling system ever devised, and the iconic Inlaid nib, introduced in 1959 on the PFM, the Pen For Men.

Swan Japan - Swan was founded in 1900 and was using the trade name for pens before Mabie Todd began exporting to Japan. In its early years Swan was one of the largest pen makers in Japan. The company produced high quality pens through the 1990s.

Tuckersharpe - The Tuckersharpe Pen Company was founded in 1952 by Percy Tucker in Richmond, Virginia. He used himself as the spokesman in some of his company's advertising. The company made inexpensive fountain and ballpoint pens claiming millions of sales.

Wahl Eversharp - Wahl Eversharp was one of the "big four" pen manufacturers in the USA in the 1920s-1940s. The company began making and marketing the highly successful Eversharp mechanical pencil in 1915 and followed with the Wahl fountain pen in 1917. The company was especially noted for its 1920s era machine turned metal pens and pencils offered in many beautiful designs.

Waterford - Waterford was founded in 1783 by William and George Penrose to "create the finest quality crystal for drinking vessels and objects of beauty for the home". About two hundred years later the company licensed to create Waterford writing instruments.

Waterman - The Waterman pen company was established in 1884 in New York City by Lewis Edson Waterman. Waterman was one of the "big four" pen makers in the United States and made many notable and collectable pen models including many early hard rubber pens, safety pens, and overlay pens. The CF model, introduced in 1953, was among the first plastic cartridge fountain pens and introduced the clip design that carries forward to current Waterman pens. The flagship MAN 100 was introduced in 1983 to celebrate the company's 100th anniversary.

Wearever - David Kahn, Inc., established in 1896 in North Bergen, New Jersey, proudly mass produced and heavily advertised its Wearever pens as affordable alternatives to the more expensive top tier brands. Wearever pens are ubiquitous finds in antique stores and pen shows.

Well - Well (made by Mitsumoto-Honten and distributed by Diamond) was a smaller Japanese pen maker from the 1920s through the 1950s.

Yotsubishi - Ishi-Shoten, also known as Ishi & Co., was established in Tokyo in 1925 by pen maker Yoshinosuke Ishii. Ishi-Shoten used the four diamond trademark, yotsubishi in Japanese, and the mark can be found on the clip top on most pens. The company ceased operations in 1984.

Glossary

Decorative Techniques

Guilloche is an engraving technique where a precise, intricate and repeated pattern is mechanically engraved into an underlying material via engine turning.

Kamakura-bori is a decorative technique done by carving patterns in wood or lacquer revealing layers of color and then polishing to finish.

Kawari-nuri, literally "free pattern," is a decorative technique where the artist is free to produce any abstract pattern in the urushi lacquer, which is then over coated in clear urushi.

Taka maki-e is a maki-e technique where the design is built up from the surface or literally "raised."

Togidashi maki-e is a maki-e technique where an urushi lacquer painting is sprinkled with gold or silver powder and then painted to fix the powder, literally "burnished."

Urushi is a high quality lacquer, containing urushiol, made from the toxic sap of the Chinese lacquer tree.

Filling Systems

Aerometric / squeeze fill pens work by removing the barrel and repeatedly squeezing a tab on the filler unit. Aerometric was the Parker Pen Company name for its squeeze filler that had a breather tube.

Blow fill pens fill by blowing into or attaching and compressing a bulb at the hole at the base of the barrel. This squeezes the ink sac, which fills as it decompresses. There is a concave depression in the top of the cap and in the bottom of the barrel and each has a hole drilled at the center. The cap can be used to lengthen the pen for this purpose.

Bulb filler pens work by repeatedly squeezing a bulb on the end of the barrel until it fills.

Button fill pens fill by pressing the button at the bottom of the barrel which bends a pressure bar that compresses the ink sac inside the barrel. The sac fills as it expands.

Capillary fill pens have a Teflon coated capillary capsule attached to the base of the nib section. It fills by putting the capsule end in the ink bottle and the perforated material inside the capsule absorbs and holds the ink. The Teflon coating keeps ink from sticking so the pen can be put back together without wiping.

Cartridge / converter pens use replaceable ink cartridges or a cartridge like device that can mechanically draw ink through the nib, called a converter.

Dip pens work as the name implies, where the nib is dipped in ink and writes until dry.

Eyedropper pens fill by unscrewing the nib section and dripping ink into the barrel. These pens were often sold with eyedroppers for this purpose. Many Japanese eyedropper pens have a shut off valve which regulates ink flow by slightly opening the end cap to allow ink flow to the section or closing it to stop.

Lever-fill pens work by pulling a lever on the barrel which pushes a bar that compresses the ink sac inside the barrel. The sac fills as it expands.

Piston fill pens work by twisting a knob on the end of the barrel that activates a mechanical piston inside drawing in ink similarly to a syringe.

Rubber diaphragm or sac plunger fill pens have a spring loaded plunger mechanism attached to a sac or diaphragm at the end of the barrel. Pumping the plunger repeatedly fills the barrel of the pen.

Touchdown / Snorkel filler pens work by pulling out the plunger, inserting the nib in ink, and quickly pushing in the plunger, compressing the ink sac inside the barrel. The sac fills as it expands. Snorkel pens add a long tube that extends from under the nib as the plunger is unscrewed. Only the tube is inserted in the ink.

Vacuum fill pens work by pulling out the plunger, inserting the nib in ink, and quickly pushing in the plunger, creating a vacuum that fills the barrel with ink. These pens fill with one downstroke.

References

Andreaslambrou.com, Lambrou Publishers website
Classicpensinc.com, © 2017 Lambrou Pens
"Collecting Japanese Pens," by Stan Klemanowicz, Pennant, Winter 2006
Fountain Pens of Japan by Andreas Lambrou and Masamichi Sunami, © 2012 Andreas Lambrou Publishers, Epping, Essex, United Kingdom
Parker "51" by David and Mark Shepherd, Surrenden Pens Limited, Brighton, UK, 2004
Parkerpen.com, Parker website
PenHero.com, PenHero.com website
Pelikan.com, Pelikan company website
Platinum-pen.co.jp, Platinum pen company website
Sheaffertarga.com, © 2012 sheaffertarga.com, Gary Ellison
Vintagepens.com, © 1997-2017 David Nishimura
Wahleversharp.com, website of the new Wahl Eversharp Pen Company
Waterman.com, Waterman website

About the Author

Jim Mamoulides was initially drawn to fountain pens through his interest in calligraphy, but did not become an avid collector until he lost a Montblanc ballpoint pen and began a search of pen stores for a replacement, discovering the fascinating world of pen collecting. His interest in the history of fountain pens led him to focus on vintage pens and his articles and photography can be found on his website PenHero.com. Jim's photographic work has been featured in the books Fountain Pens of Japan and Collecting Pens, the Pennant, Pen World, DuPont Registry, Antique Traders Collector, Antique Week, and Connecticut Cottages & Gardens magazines, and manufacturer websites such as Classic Pens, Cleo Skribent, and Sheaffer. He has been interviewed numerous times about pen collecting, including an interview for O The Oprah Magazine.

www.ingramcontent.com/pod-product-compliance
Lightning Source LLC
Chambersburg PA
CBHW041515220426
43668CB00002B/27